W9-BGW-074

The Kid
DICTIONARY

★ ★

Hilarious Words to Describe the Indescribable Things Kids Do

ERIC RUHALTER

 sourcebooks

Published by Sourcebooks, Inc.

P.O. Box 4410, Naperville, Illinois 60567-4410

(630) 961-3900

Fax: (630) 961-2168

www.sourcebooks.com

Library of Congress Cataloging-in-Publication Data

Ruhalter, Eric.

  The kid dictionary : hilarious words to describe the indescribable things kids do / Eric Ruhalter.

     p. cm.

  (pbk. : alk. paper) 1. Children—Humor. 2. American wit and humor—Dictionaries. 3. Parents—Humor. I. Title.

  PN6231.C32R84 2012

  818'.602—dc23

2011035366

Printed and bound in the United States of America.

VP 10 9 8 7 6 5 4 3 2 1

This book is dedicated to my children, Jaxen, Maya, and Crosby, who inspire me in ways I could never describe (until recently).

And to Kara, my wife and best friend, who speaks my language and believes in me even when I don't.

Acknowledgments

Getting this book off the ground was no small chore, and I offer sincere thanks to everyone who helped me, encouraged me, and tolerated me throughout the process. To name a few—my wife, Kara; my wonderful children; and my friends Erl Rome and Beth Chandler, Jon Mace, Jon and Heather Whelan, Margaret Noonan and Michael Tatlow, Scott Wythe, Beth Feldman, and Robert Battles. Also to Shana Drehs at Sourcebooks, for being willing to give my crazy idea a chance. For some bits of inspiration along the way, I acknowledge the Benjets, Kilgores, Kubins, Whelans, O'Sullivans, Hamiltons, Gardeners, Hubers, Carrions, Dannas, and Molinaros, as well as Bill Lewis, Margaret Whitener, Tim Weathington, Jill McAdam, Wendy Boyce, Kim Kinrade, James Viotto, and Barbara Dundas.

And, as ever, I acknowledge my mom and dad and brothers, who never ridiculed me for thinking differently. Or haven't recently. At least not to my face.

Introduction

One day a few years ago, I was at a five-year-old girl's birthday party with my daughter. All the family and friends were gathered around the birthday girl to sing "Happy Birthday" and eat cake. We got to the end of the song, and as the little girl paused to make her wish before blowing out the candles, a boy leaned in beside her and blew them out for her. Mayhem ensued. Having seen this same scenario go down many times, I thought, "There really ought to be a word for this." I came up with the verb *wishjack* (WISH-jak): to blow out the candles on another child's birthday cake.

On another occasion I saw my son Jaxen looking in the mirror at the gap where one of his teeth used to be. He clutched in his hand a crisp, new dollar bill, courtesy of the Tooth Fairy. "What do you think?" I asked. And he replied,

"I think if I knock all my teeth out, I'll be rich!" And I thought, "There should be a word for that, too. Perhaps a cross between the words *orthodontist* and *entrepreneur*." And thus was born *orthodontrepreneur* (or-thoh-DAHN-truh-pre-noor), noun: a child who wants to knock out all of his own teeth in the interest of a hefty payday from the Tooth Fairy.

Many more words followed. Soon there were enough for this book. And thanks to the antics at my house and everywhere I take my kids, new words are inspired every single day. There's truly no end in sight, so please stay tuned for more Kid Definitions from *The Kid Dictionary*.

FEELABUSTER

(FEEHL-uh-buhs-tur) v :

To pat down your toddler before she leaves a play date at someone else's house to make sure she isn't stealing any toys.

Newton's
EXCEPTION

(NOO-tuhn's ek-SEPT-shun) n :

The explanation to one's child that a helium balloon lost outside is never coming back.

DETASTE

(dee-TAYST) v :

To harbor a deep hatred and disgust for a food you have never tried.

fig. I

ERADICRAP

ee-RA-di-crap v :

To purge your playroom of old toys when your kids aren't around to protest.

"FULLISH"

(FUHL-ish) adj :

Too full to eat more carrots, yet fully prepared to consume an ice-cream sundae.

INVISIBOOBOO

(in-VIZ-uh-boo-boo) n :

The site on a child's body where you unnecessarily applied a bandage to appease him when he got hurt, even though no blood ever appeared.

Trashcannaissance
MISSION

(trash-CAN-a-sintz MI-shun) n :

Routine exercise of retrieving
important items from
the garbage (e.g., silverware,
TV remote, car keys),
which your toddler
threw away for fun.

DOVE CRY

(DUHV CRYE) v :

To cry out for a sudden, emphatic, and immediate need for a towel, which overcomes a child when soap gets in her eyes.

(Also referred to as DIAL 911.)

Toyphoon

(toy-FOON) n :

Routine recreational activity
of children that leaves their
playroom looking as if it were
decimated by a hurricane.

PEEQUEL

(PEE-kwuhl) n :

A child's need to pee while driving in the car, ten minutes after leaving the highway rest stop, where he insisted that he didn't have to go.

SHOTTUP

(shot-UP) v :

To neglect to mention to your child that her visit to the doctor will yield not only a sticker and a lollipop but also a sharp needle jabbed into her arm.

POODINI

(poo-DEE-nee) n :

A baby who has learned how
to escape from his crib.

Monopolooze

(moh-NAH-puh-looz) v :

To strategically lose a board game against an unsportsmanlike child.

Blubberish

(BLUH-bur-ish) n :

The incomprehensible, breathless stammering of a crying child trying to tell you what happened to her.

fig. 2

Victory
LAMENTATION

(VIC-tor-ee
LA-men-TAY-shun) n :

The tantrum that ensues when an unsportsmanlike child loses a board game (to a parent who failed to monopolooze).

Crydentity CRISIS

(crye-DEN-ti-tee
CRY-sis) n :

Silence that falls over a group
of parents at a play date
when a cry is heard from
the next room and they are
all determining whether the
crying child is theirs.

MADDRESS

(mad-DRES) v :

To refer to a child by his first and middle name in a stern voice, thus denoting that he's about to get in trouble.

BUNNYCOMB

(BUHN-ee-cohm) v :

To frantically search the house
for a toddler's favorite stuffed animal
to avoid a meltdown.

Fecalarity

(fee-cuhl-EHR-i-tee) n :

The comic force that causes a child to laugh herself to the floor at the mere mention of the word *poop*.

"DECRAPITATE"

(de-CRAP-uh-tayt) v :

To debunk the foolish myths that your kids' ignorant friends utter.

Freak of
NURTURE

(FREEK UHV NUR-chuhr) n :

A child who, without any prompting, wants to eat well-balanced meals and avoid junk food, gets enough sleep and exercise, and realizes the value of his education.

Shhh...

HYPOCRITICIZE

(hip-oh-CRIT-i-SYZE) v :

To yell at your kids to keep their voices down.

SHRAM

(SHRAM) v :

To try to put on shoes with the laces still tied from the last time they were worn.

DADUATION

(DAD-joo-AY-shun) n :

The painful realization that you are quickly and irreversibly turning into your parents.

STOCKTEASE

(STAHK-teez) n :

A child who lets you buy large quantities of her favorite food and then suddenly decides that she doesn't like it anymore.

VEGEVICT

(vedj-ee-VIKT) v :

To adamantly insist that food you do
not like be removed from your plate
completely and immediately.

Droppler EFFECT

(DRAHP-lur e-FEKT) n :

The prolonged uneasy feeling parents experience when watching their toddler walk across the kitchen, carrying a full glass of juice.

ASSAULT
and BATTER

(uh-SAWLT AND BA-tur) v :

To be informed by your child at 8:30
in the morning that he volunteered you
to prepare forty cupcakes for his class's
holiday party that day.

WE'LL SEE

(WEE-uhl SEE) interj :

No.

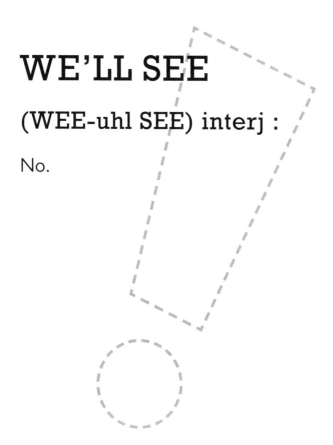

SKLEEVE

(SKLEEV) v :

To force one's head through the armhole of a shirt.

fig. 3

Nicktronize

(NIK-truh-nyze) v :

To feign belief in Santa Claus with hopes of a bigger Christmas payload.

(See EASTERBLUFFING.)

PASTOVERS

(PAZ-toh-vurs) n :

Uneaten food items that come home in
the lunch box.

woof!

ROVERTURE

(ROW-vuhr-chuhr) n :

A child's discussion of what kind of pet she would like after the current one dies.

meow!

Phantomolition

(FAN-tuh-muh-LI-shun) n :

When something gets broken but no
one did it.

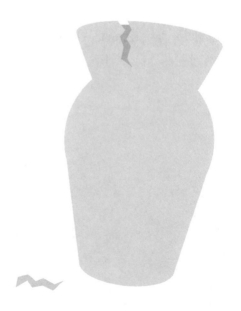

BOOTALITY

(boo-TAL-uh-tee) n :

A child's notion that "keep your hands to yourself" does not preclude him from kicking someone.

SIBROIDERY

(sib-ROY-dehr-ee) n :

An article of hand-me-down clothing with the older sibling's name or initials on it.

MACOUSTICS

(mah-COO-stiks) n :

The frequency of a mother's voice that her children find so easy to ignore.

GUESTILENCE

(GHEST-i-lintz) n :

A parent's innate preference that her child's play date be held at the other kid's house.

PUPPYMOON

(PUH-pee-moon) n :

The extremely brief period of time immediately after adopting a pet when your children live up to their promise of performing the chores associated with caring for said pet.

fig. 4

CHAPTURN

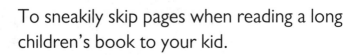

(CHAP-turn) v :

To sneakily skip pages when reading a long
children's book to your kid.

CHAPTURKEY

(chap-TUR-kee) n :

A parent who gets caught skipping pages when reading a long children's book to his or her kid.

Apologuise

(ah-PAHL-oh-guyz) v :

To force your children to say they're sorry, knowing full well how worthless and insincere the apology will be.

ADRENALAD

(ah-DREHN-uh-lad) n :

A child who will never ever under any circumstances admit that he is tired.

CRESTICKLE

(CRES-ti-kuhl) n :

Smear of kids' toothpaste all over the
bathroom sink, counter, and mirror.

POPPALARITY

(PAH-pal-LAHR-ih-tee) n :

High approval rating that pushover fathers receive from their children for letting them watch more TV, eat more junk, stay up later, etc.

CARNIVOID

(KAR-nuh-voyd) v :

To alter your driving route when the kids are in the car so as not to pass by a carnival that is in town.

SWISS DISS

(SWIS DIS) v :

To serve a grilled cheese sandwich with the burnt side down so your child will not reject it.

REST RHUMBA

(REST RUHM-buh) v :

To indicate that you have to use the bathroom by fidgeting, squirming, clutching, and leg-crossing.

SNOTSAM

(SNAHT-suhm) n :

Any unidentified sticky
or slimy substance.

fig. 5

CLANDESDINE

(klan-DES-dyne) v :

To hide from one's child while eating a cookie so he doesn't ask for one too.

SANDROID

(SAN-droyd) n :

A child at the beach who is completely unfazed by sand caking every crevice in her body.

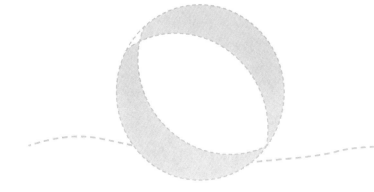

SPORTSMANSKIP

(SPORTZ-man-skip) n :

A child's loss of interest in a sport two weeks into the sixteen-week program he begged you to sign him up and outfit him for (nonrefundably so, of course).

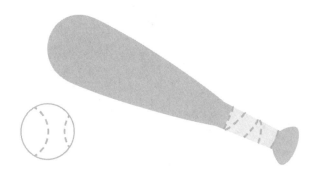

Gag Rag

(GAG RAG) n :

The towel placed over a child's pillow when she goes to sleep after having thrown up.

UPTITUDE

(UHP-tih-tood) n :

The intense desire to be the one who presses the button in an elevator.

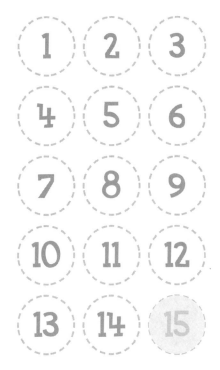

SHMAGIGGLE

(shma-GIG-uhl) v :

To laugh at something that you find not even remotely funny to appease a young child who thinks he's a comedian.

XOX

(ZAHKS) v :

To intentionally lose a game
of tic-tac-toe to a four-year-old.

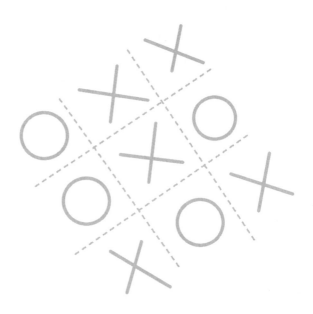

CARDBOREDOM

(card-BOHR-duhm) n :

A child's tendency to ignore a new toy and instead play with the box it came in.

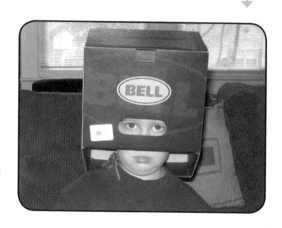

fig. 6

DINTERCOURSE

(DIN-tur-cors) n :

State of revulsion evoked when, heaven forbid, two different food items on a plate touch.

GARBOFLAGE

(GAHR-boh-flajh) v :

To hide a piece of your child's artwork under other trash in the wastebasket so she doesn't catch you throwing it away.

SHAMPEST

(sham-PEST) n :

A child who will climb a flight of stairs and barge in on Mom in the shower to ask her for a glass of milk when Dad is in the kitchen.

HOARDGAME

(HORD-gaym) n :

A long-neglected plaything that a child develops a sudden interest in when Mom says she's going to get rid of it.

PLAYBACK

(PLAY-bak) v :

To force your child to endure a play date with a child he doesn't wish to play with, because you owe the child's mom a favor.

Harrask

(huh-RASK) v :

To persist in asking again and again for permission to do something with hopes that the answer will change from no to yes.

PETSWAP

(pet-SWAHP) v :

To attempt, often ill fatedly, to secretly replace a pet (e.g., turtle, goldfish, hamster) who has died.

CENSURF

(SEN-surf) v :

To quickly change a channel when happening upon a scene that is completely inappropriate for your kids when they are in the room.

SHTUNKER

(SHTUN-kur) n :

A child who puts something in the toilet that doesn't belong there.

fig. 7

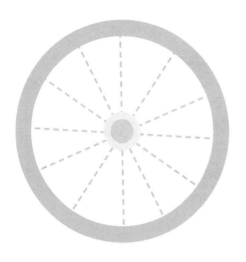

SCHWINNCIDENT

(SHWIN-suh-dent) n :

When a child leaves a bicycle on the
ground in the driveway behind the car.

PEDALSTOOL

(PED-uhl-stool) n :

The over-the-top praise heaped on a kid
when she learns to ride a bike.

JUVENOMICS

(JOO-ve-NAHM-iks) n :

A child's faulty understanding of the value of money (e.g., he can purchase a beach house with the fistful of nickels and pennies in his piggy bank).

COOPHORIA

(koo-FOR-ee-uh) n :

The opiatelike contentment
grown-ups feel with a baby
in their arms.

WINNERGY

(WIN-ur-jee) n :

The notion that every kid on every sports team, regardless of how well or poorly the team did, should receive a trophy.

JINGLEBERRY

(JING-guhl-BEHR-ee) n :

A holiday song whose lyrics have been changed to incorporate potty talk and other themes contrary to the season the songs are intended to celebrate.

BROWNDOG

(BROWN-dawg) n :

A baby who poops in a fresh diaper before you've even fastened the adhesive tabs.

FOOFONT

(foo-FAHNT) n :

A child who still has bed head
around dinnertime.

fig. 8

TOKENCRUNCH

(TOH-ken-kruntch) v :

To eat only as many bowls of cereal as it takes to get to the toy in the box.

SUPPERCATE

(SUHP-ur-kayt) v :

To take two bites of dinner and
then request dessert.

Snoot

(SNOOT) v :

To suck in rather than blow out when blowing your nose.

NODOZER

(NOH-doh-zur) n :

A baby who falls asleep in the stroller or car seat but springs wide awake the instant you transfer her to her crib.

IMPOLERT

(im-poh-LURT) n :

A child's indiscreet call of attention in public to a stranger's physical abnormality (e.g., "Hey, look! He's only got *one leg*!").

SUBTATTLE

(SUB-ta-tuhl) v :

To reprimand a sibling in a
loud voice with the primary
goal of alerting Mom and Dad.

WISHJACK

(WISH-jak) v :

To blow out the candles on another child's birthday cake.

fig. 9

KIDDLES

(KI-duhls) n :

Crumbs and debris found in the creases of your automobile upholstery when you remove your child's car seat.

WHYARRHEA

(WYE-uh-REE-uh) n :

An inquisitive toddler's chain of questions rattled off in rapid-fire succession.

Doughliberate

(doh-LIB-ur-ayt) v :

To spend an inordinate amount of time deciding which crappy prizes to cash in your tickets for at an arcade or school fair.

DISHCOVETRY

(dish-CUHV-it-ree) n :

When a child finds your dinner more pleasing to the palate than her own.

YUPPING

(YUH-ping) v :

To acknowledge what your two-year-old is communicating to you when you have no idea what he's trying to say.

INSTANSOMNIA

(in-stan-SAHM-nee-uh) n :

A child's snap assessment that she can't sleep about twenty seconds after she lies down for bed.

NUTLER

(NUHT-lur) n :

A clumsy mobile toddler whose head is just about the height of the average adult male's crotch.

fig. 10

FREAKALL

(FREEK-awl) n :

A child's rock-solid
memory of things you
really want him to forget.

Radardianship

(ray-DAHR-dee-uhn-ship) n :

A child's notion that it is her parents'
responsibility to know the precise
whereabouts of any of her things
at any given time.

DAWDEFY

(DAW-duh-fye) v :

When a child shows power by doing what you asked as sloooowly as possible.

SPONGEBOGGED

(SPUNJ-bahgd) adj :

Unable to record a movie because your DVR is filled with kids' shows.

NOPEN

(NOH-pen) v :

To witness your kid pulling the car door handle just as you're trying to automatically unlock the doors, such that her door remains locked, forcing you to lock and unlock again (and repeat).

POODOODLE

(poo-DOO-duhl) v :

To paint, color, give a haircut to, or
otherwise deface the family pet.

MALLOWMINE

(MAHL-oh-myne) v :

To eat only the marshmallows out of
a sweetened breakfast cereal.

THUMBLE

(THUM-buhl) v :

To speak incoherently with one's fingers in his mouth.

fig. 11

"PARDUNCE"

(PAR-duntz) n :

A child who is completely incapable of taking even the remotest responsibility for his actions.

SKOFFSPRING

(SKOF-spring) n :

An adolescent child who's reached the conclusion that his parents are stupid.

BEANBAGGER

(BEAN-ba-gur) n :

A child who tries to smuggle her
vegetables from the dinner table to
the wastebasket in the bathroom.

Rugrat RACE

(RUG-rat RAYSE) n :

The reality that you're going to be at least a little bit tired from the moment you have your first child until your last child moves out.

CRESTY EYED

(CRESS-tee IDE) adj :

Too sleepy to brush one's teeth.

SHRAPTURE

(SHRAP-chuhr) n :

The agony worn by a child with a splinter in his foot that results not from the splinter but from fearful anticipation of the tweezers.

KINSULTATION

(KIN-suhl-TAY-shun) n :

The act of asking Mom for permission to do something because Dad said no, or vice versa.

RANTONESE

(RAN-tuhn-EEZ) n :

The language consisting of the huffing, harrumphing, and muttering of an angry child who just got punished.

SHIRTURBED

(shur-TURBD) adj :

Annoyed at having just received an
article of clothing as a present.

fig. 12

MANAJERK

(MAN-uh-jurk) n :

Coach of a kids' sports team who is extremely partial and preferential to his own child and can't see that your kid is really the star.

DISSUCTION

(dis-SUHK-shun) n :

The act of sifting through a vacuum-cleaner bag to rescue a toy that got sucked up.

STORNADO

(store-NAY-doh) n :

A child who is a complete nightmare to bring to the store because he has to touch everything and/or relentlessly try to get you to buy him something.

WARDRODEO

(war-DROH-dee-OH) n :

The difficult chore of dressing a
squirming, uncooperative toddler.

SCAMPLIFIER

(SKAM-pluh-FYE-ur) n :

A child who feels the need to shout when talking to someone who's just inches away.

HAIRRICANE

(HAIR-uh-kayn) n :

A girl's knotty, messy hair and the ensuing tantrums that erupt when her mother tries to comb it out.

SPITSICLE

(SPIT-si-cuhl) n :

The string of drool that extends from a baby's mouth to his pants.

fig. 13

"GRENEGG"

(greh-NEG) v :

To whimper and retch while tasting a new food before it is anywhere near your mouth.

NOPEFULNESS

(NOHP-ful-nes) n :

A child's knee-jerk compulsion to disagree with everything her parents say.

SCARBER

(SCAR-bur) n :

A kid who takes it upon herself to cut her own hair or that of a younger sibling or pet.

SEMICAPITATE

(SEM-ee-KAP-uh-tayt) v :

To remove a child's shirt when the neck hole is a touch too small to fit comfortably over his head, thus inflicting great trauma and pain on his ears, chin, cheeks, nose, and/or eyebrows.

SEPTEMBILATION

(sep-TEM-bil-AY-shun) n :

The utter glee that washes over stay-at-home parents when their kids return to school after a challenging summer.

SLOBBERTIZE

(SLAH-bur-tyze) v :

To use spit on a napkin to clean something off your kid's face when you're not near a sink.

KIDGILANTE

(KID-juh-LAN-tee) n :

A child who makes a point of alerting you when you're doing something that is contrary to the law (e.g., going through a yellow light in the car).

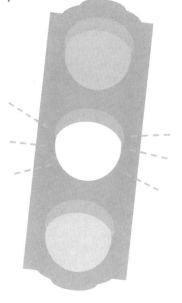

Regurgitighten

(ri-GUR-ji-TYE-tuhn) v :

To brace yourself after ascertaining that your ill child is about to barf on you.

fig. 14

LEFTOAF

(lef-TOHF) n :

A parent whose diet consists largely of foods her children don't finish.

KINTERPRET

(kin-TUR-prit) v :

To feel compelled to repeat or translate everything your kids say when you talk to other grown-ups.

SLEEZSTOCK

(SLEEZ-stahk) v :

To put a half-eaten piece of food back on a buffet platter.

BUFFOODERY

(buh-FOOD-ur-ee) n :

The swiftness with which a child returns to eating with his mouth open after you scold him to keep it closed.

RERUNT

(REE-ruhnt) n :

A child with the ability to watch the same episodes of a TV show over and over again without ever getting bored of them.

SHAMPOON

(sham-POON) v :

To get out of the shower without rinsing the suds from your hair.

WRAPPETITE

(RAP-uh-tyte) n :

A child's interest in eating something because of the allure of its snazzy packaging.

HAMPURGLAR

(ham-PUR-glur) n :

A parent who lets her child wear an article of clothing out of the dirty pile.

BLUBBERNECKER

(BLUH-bur-NEK-ur) n :

A stranger who stands and gawks when a child is having a tantrum.

ASSPLOSION

(ass-PLOH-zhuhn) n :

When a baby poops with such tremendous force that the diaper cannot contain it and the poop shoots all the way up the back.

CHARMANGLED

(shar-MAHNG-eld) adj :

The discombobulated state of a roll of toilet paper that's been unfurled and recoiled several times by a toddler who treats it like a party favor.

fig. 15

GRAVITOYS

(GRAV-ih-toyz) n :

Playthings that are light enough to be brought out into the living room and scattered about but too heavy to pick up and put away.

MESSTIBULE

(MES-ti-byool) n :

The clutter of coats, mittens, shoes, hats, backpacks, etc., that litters the area around the front door after a bunch of kids enter the house.

P.M. PEE

(pee-em PEE) n :

A child's need to go to the bathroom multiple times after she's tucked in to bed.

ARITHMATRIX

(uh-rith-MAY-triks) n :

The point at which the difficulty of your child's math assignments surpasses your own mathematical ability.

$$72x^3 \div 37y^4 = ?$$

FLOTSIP

(FLAHT-sip) v :

To drink from your kid's cup, only to have a chunk of whatever you most recently fed him assault your mouth.

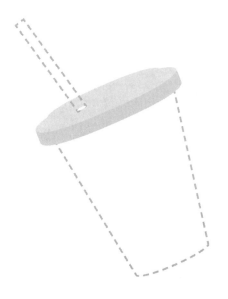

MOMIKAZE

(MAHM-uh-KAH-zee) n :

A mother whose children push her to the very brink of her sanity.

YELEGATE

(YEL-uh-gayt) v :

To scold another person's child.

LESSAY

(LES-ay) n :

A composition written by a
middle schooler that is not
one single letter longer than it
needs to be.

FILTHLETE

(FILTH-leet) n :

A child who goes out of his way to make sure his sports uniform gets as dirty as possible.

fig. 16

"MUNCHKISS"

(MUNTCH-kis) v :

To eat the icing off a doughnut or cupcake and then put it back.

BEDDISON

(BED-uh-suhn) v :

To let a child fall asleep in your
bed and then very carefully
move her back to her own bed.

POTTYSITTER

(PAH-tee-SI-tur) n :

A parent who is forced to take his toddler with him into the bathroom because the toddler cannot be left alone.

DISROBIENTATE

(dis-ROH-bee-uhn-tayt) v :

To intentionally leave your toddler's half-removed shirt over her face at pre-bath-time to distract her so you can remove her pants.

PANSHEE

(PAN-shee) n :

A child who would rather walk around with excrement in his pants than cooperate with potty training.

ANKLER

(AYN-klur) n :

A child who clings to a parent's leg on the first day of preschool.

SCREAMORSE

(skree-MORS) n :

The regret that ensues immediately upon giving your child a toy that makes noise.

GARMINX

(GAHR-minks) n :

A little girl who feels compelled to change her clothes fifty times a day.

Turd ALERT

(TURD uh-LURT) n :

The astounding horror a parent experiences upon finding a child's number two in the toilet, unflushed and unaccompanied by toilet paper.

KODICK

(COH-dik) n :

The child who refuses to cooperate in the taking of a family photograph.

fig. 17

PUMPOOZLE

(pum-POO-zuhl) v :

To borrow Dad's car and return it with an empty gas tank.

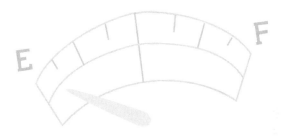

SANTASTROPHE

(san-TAS-truh-fee) n :

A parent's misconception that her baby will enjoy being handed to an enormous, white-haired, long-bearded, bespectacled stranger in a blood-red fuzzy suit for a Christmas photo.

Mistorical
PERSPECTIVE

(MIS-tor-i-kuhl
pur-SPEK-tiv) n :

Recollections of your youth you tell to your children, leaving out any and all incidents of underage drinking, drug experimentation, and sexual promiscuity.

CURDLER

(KURD-lur) n :

A sippy cup once containing milk that has been lost under a piece of furniture for several weeks.

HOPSPUCKER

(HAHPS-puh-kur) n :

Reaction on a child's face to his
first sip of beer.

NOCTHIRSTAL

(nahk-THUR-stuhl) n :

A child's need for a bedside glass of water that she never, ever drinks but frequently spills.

Orthodontrepreneur

(or-thoh-DAHN-truh-pre-noor) n :

A child who wants to knock out all of his own teeth in the interest of a hefty payday from the Tooth Fairy.

fig. 18

N.R.A.-
DOLESCENCE

(en-ar-A-doh-LES-entz) n :

The period when children, predominantly male children, discover the playtime fun associated with pretending to kill people.

Threemageddon

(three-muh-GHED-in) n :

The supposed hellfire and brimstone that would erupt should an annoyed mother reach the third digit when counting to three to prompt a child to get his act together

(e.g., "One!…Two!…*Two and a half!*").

INFLAGING

(in-FLAY-jing) n :

A child's tendency to insist she is older than she really is.

THREEQUELS

(THREE-kwuls) n :

The three books you read to your kids after you read them the "last" book before bed.

RESEMBULLATE

(ri-ZEM-buhl-ayt) v :

To unnecessarily assess which parent a
newborn baby looks like.

KINDERWARP

(KIN-dur-warp) n :

A child's time management logic by which he thinks he can watch a movie, play a video game, and have cocoa, because bedtime is at 8:00 p.m. and it's only 7:53.

SLEDENTARY

(SLED-en-tehr-ee) adj :

Being so bundled up to face the winter elements that a child cannot move.

fig. 19

SANDSWITCH

(SAND-swich) v :

To change your mind about what you want your parents to put in your lunch box after it's much too late—often when at the bus stop.

MISCROSS

(mis-CROS) v :

To fail to take the precaution of looking both ways until you're halfway across the street.

ASSIBITION

(ASS-uh-BI-shun) n :

Immodest stage during which young boys see nothing wrong with taking their pants down to their ankles to pee in a public restroom.

KEGULATE

(KEG-yoo-layt) v :

To ponder the future cost of your child's college education while recollecting that mostly what you did there was drink beer.

ETHIOPULENCE

(EETH-ee-OH-pyoo-lentz) n :

State of good fortune neglected by every child with a roof over her head and food to eat

(e.g., Parent: "Do you know how lucky you are to have a home to live in and to never have to go to bed hungry?"
Child: "Do you know that Jake has the new iPhone?!").

FRIENDSOMNIA

(frend-SOM-nee-uh) n :

The lack of sleep that occurs at
a sleepover.

DISDRESS

(dis-DRES) n :

Unfashionable looks achieved by toddlers who are just learning to dress themselves.

(Also adj : "IN DISDRESS")

fig. 20

SCOOBUNGLE

(skoo-BUNG-uhl) v :

To prematurely bite off the bottom tip of an ice-cream cone on a hot summer day.

Discoolification

(dis-COOL-i-fuh-KAY-shun) n :

A parent's gradual transformation from being his child's hero to being his greatest source of embarrassment.

"Cyclomagnetism"

(SY-cloh-MAG-nuh-tiz-uhm) n :

Irregular gravitational pull that causes a kid riding a bike for the first time to veer into trees, parked cars, and other large stationary objects.

Disheart-to-heart
TALK

(dis-HART-too-HART tawk) n :

Disappointing responses to your sincerest proclamations of love for your children

(e.g., Father (earnestly): "I will love you and take care of you and protect you forever and ever, my sweetest little princess."
Three-year-old daughter: "Daddy, you have hair in your nose!").

A.M. FREEZE

(ay-em FREEZ) n :

The early morning hope, upon hearing a stirring infant or toddler, that if you stay perfectly still and quiet he will go back to sleep. (Never in the history of parentkind has this worked).

SHITISTICS

(shi-TIS-tiks) n :

The incredibly inaccurate stats an eight-year-old spouts while watching a sporting event.

fig. 21

REWHINE

(REE-wyne) n :

The short, light whine that a child emits immediately after you scold her, "Stop whining!"

Ridicrimand

(ree-DIK-ruh-mand) v :

To make a preposterously empty threat

(e.g., "If you don't stop that right now…no more air!").

BROFITTI

(broh-FEE-tee) n :

The act of scribbling with permanent marker on the face of a younger sibling.

NAPFUSION

(nap-FYOO-zhuhn) n :

The dilemma of whether to wake a
toddler who falls asleep at 4 p.m.

TANGLET

(TANG-let) n :

Impossibly complex knot created by a child in the early stages of learning to tie his shoes.

LULLACRY

(LUL-uh-crye) n :

The dramatic pause between
a child sustaining an injury and
beginning to wail.

DRINKLE

(DRIN-kuhl) n :

The liquid burst emitted
from the little straw when
a toddler grips her juice
box too tightly.

SPOONAMI

(spoo-NAH-mee) n :

The aftermath in your silverware drawer subsequent to letting your three-year-old empty the dishwasher cutlery basket.

Jemima CLAUSE

(je-MYE-muh clawz) n :

Leniency in the dietary code that allows for classification of chocolate-chip pancakes smothered with syrup and whipped cream as breakfast rather than dessert.

STONEWAIL

(STOHN-wayl) v :

To strategically display no emotion in response to your child's public tantrum.

fig. 22

PAMPERATIONS

(pam-pur-AY-shuns) n :

The twisting, squirming, and kicking a baby performs to make it as difficult as possible to change his diaper.

DISSCRIPT

(dis-KRIPT) v :

To flub one's single line in
a kindergarten play.

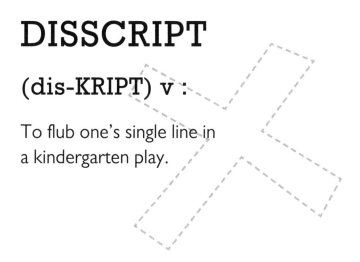

DEFRAMATION

(DE-fruh-MAY-shun) n :

The sharp decline in photos and videos taken of your second child relative to the amount taken of your first.

NINTENDOID

(nin-TEN-doyd) n :

A child who is helplessly and disturbingly addicted to video games.

Shkoff

(SHKAWF) v :

To remove one's shoes without untying the laces.

BUFFERT

(BUF-urt) n :

The distance a child at the dinner table insists on keeping between himself and a plate of food he does not wish to eat.

DISSLACKSIA

(dis-LAKS-ee-uh) n :

A young girl's insistence that she always wear a dress, never pants.

KEDTUSIONS

(ked-TOO-zhuhns) n :

Kicks to the face sustained while trying to tie a toddler's shoes.

Tooned
OUT

(TOOND OWT) adj :

Being in a catatonic state while seated before a television.

fig. 23

NIGHTCAPPETITE

(nyte-CAP-uh-tyte) n :

The sudden-hunger portion of a child's bedtime procrastination ritual.

OVERBUB

(OH-vur-buhb) v :

To waste liquid soap by dispensing it onto hands and promptly rinsing it off without creating a lather.

POLUTENESS

(poh-LOOT-nes) n :

A child's ability to say "please," "thank you," and/or "I'm sorry" without the slightest trace of sincerity.

KNICK-KNOCK

(NICK-nahk) v :

To riddle a grown-up with a lengthy series of impossibly tedious knock-knock jokes.

(e.g., "Knock, knock."
"Who's there?"
"Ball."
"Ball who?"
"Basketball!"
…
"Knock, knock.").

WANTIZONTAL

(WAHN-tiz-AHN-tuhl) adj :

Lying on the floor, body stiffened, and screaming at the top of your lungs after not getting your way.

fig. 24

JEZEBUCK

(JEZ-uh-buhk) n :

A toddler who peels off his clothes at an inappropriate venue such as a stuffy, ornate religious celebration.

TRANSPORTOT

(TRANZ-poor-TAHT) v :

To carry a sleeping toddler from her car seat to her bed without waking her, a practice often complicated by the need to remove her shoes and coat.

SILLABUSTER

(SIL-uh-buhs-tur) n :

A child who recently learned to talk and feels the need to do so continuously for hours with little or no effort to make any kind of sense.

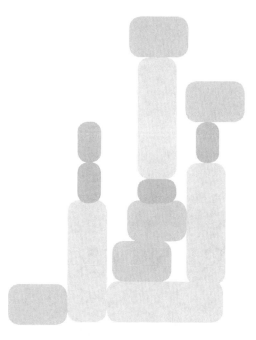

FLOORCLOSE

(flor-CLOHZ) v :

To obstruct a main thoroughfare in the
house with a shoddily constructed tower
of blocks.

Wich
HUNTER

(WICH HUHN-tur) n :

A child with an intense aversion to bread crusts.

RAMPAPER

(RAM-pay-pur) v :

To ferociously shred through the gift wrap on a present with no regard for the festive design or the time and care that went into wrapping it.

CHURCHKLE

(CHURCH-kuhl) n :

The chain reaction of laughter among children in a place or at a time when they should be quiet and reverent.

WEEBELLION

(wee-BEL-ee-yuhn) n :

When a child manages to wear down his parents and get his way.

HUMILIYAY

(hyoo-MIL-ee-YAY) v :

To cheer at your kid's sporting event with enough zeal to embarrass her.

Goon
CONTROL

(GOON cuhn-TROHL) v :

To attempt to subtly steer your child away from a friendship with a kid you do not like or do not trust, or whose parents are crack-headed idiots.

WETSOXITY

(wet-SAHKS-i-tee) n :

The magnetic-like force that draws children not wearing boots into puddles.

fig. 25

SCOOZER

(SKOO-zur) n :

A child who only has something to say to you when you're on the phone or in the bathroom.

LULLABYEBYE

(LUHL-uh-bye-bye) n :

The long, delicate, gradual process of sneaking out of the bed of your toddler who will not go to sleep unless you lie down with him.

About the Author

Eric Ruhalter studied economics at Dickinson College, where he learned, first and foremost, that he's not especially interested in the theories and principles of economics. So rather than study, he began spending most of his time writing. Don't tell his father.

Ruhalter currently resides in New Jersey with his lovely wife, Kara, and their three kids who used to defy description. He works for AMC Television in New York City.